ANYONE CAN DRAW PEOPLE

EASY STEP-BY-STEP DRAWING TUTORIAL FOR KIDS, TEENS, AND BEGINNERS.

Book 1

Aspiring artist's guide: people

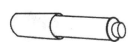

Anyone can draw people
Easy step-by-step drawing tutorial for kids, teens, and beginners. How to learn to draw people. Book 1
Aspiring artist's guide: people
2021
Julia Smith

HOW TO USE A BOOK

Draw step-by-step, following the graphic instructions. Periodically look a few steps ahead to understand what exactly you are drawing now (which part of the character), and how it'll look in the finished version.

The lessons in this book are arranged from easy to difficult so that your drawing skills develop gradually.

If you didn't succeed the first time, don't be discouraged! Think about the mistakes you made and try drawing again. Even professional artists don't always manage to draw the drawings they have in mind the first time.

YOU NEED:

Blank sheet of paper. Even notebooks or journals will do.

A pencil. Make sure that you have many pencils.

Pencil sharpener. Pencils should always be sharpened to make good lines.

Good-quality eraser. The erasers on the pencil wear out very quickly, so use a separate rubber eraser.

Colored markers or pencils. You can trace the outline of your drawing with a thin felt-tip pen and then color in.

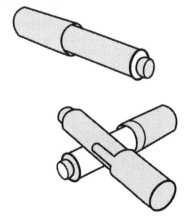

TABLE OF CONTENTS

DRAWING TIPS FOR NEWBIES

IF IT IS DIFFICULT TO SKETCH

HOW TO PERSONALIZE YOUR DRAWINGS

DO YOU WANT TO TAKE A BOOK ON A TRIP?

HOW TO MAKE A SIMPLE POSTCARD

PAINTING ON PEBBLES

GAME: "DRAW AND PASS"

DIFFICULTY LEVEL: LIGHT

DIFFICULTY LEVEL: MIDDLE

DRAWING TIPS FOR NEWBIES

Draw on different surfaces. Don't always use just plain A4 paper. Draw on notebook sheets, on the sidewalk, or in a small notebook. This will help you focus on what is important: when you have a small space for drawing, you need to develop imagination, and in order to fill a large space correctly, you should arrange everything so that it doesn't seem empty.

Periodically look at your drawing through a mirror. Thus, you can see your drawing as if with different eyes and notice the flaws. This tip helps a lot when painting portraits.

Use different materials: pencils of different thicknesses and hardness, pens (plain and helium), felt-tip pens, colored pencils, charcoal, and so on.
This will help you get a feel for the peculiarities of working with this or that instrument. And choose your favorite.

IF IT IS DIFFICULT TO SKETCH

Lean the printed sheet against the window (on a bright sunny day).

Place a blank sheet of paper over the drawing. The printed sheet will show through the blank sheet.

Sketch the outlines of the character. Then you can color and add your details.

If the lines are crooked, circle the drawing several times. The lines will get thicker and look smoother. Start tracing in short strokes, gradually aligning the line.

HOW TO PERSONALIZE YOUR DRAWINGS

Create emotions for your characters. Look at yourself in the mirror. Pretend you are fun, sad, or surprised. Note that your facial features change. Remember how the lips, eyes, and eyebrows change. Try to produce these emotions for your characters.

What makes you sad, happy, or surprised? The same can change your character's emotions. Think about what item can change the mood of your character. Add it.

Don't forget the background. Think about where your character usually goes and draw that place. What items can be found in this place? Drawings with backgrounds look more interesting and realistic. But don't do too much detail in the background because it can distract from the main drawing.

Design and draw your character, and give it a name. For example, the pirate captain Jack.

Accessories. For example, if it's a pirate, he'll look better with a hat and a sword.

Exaggeration of characteristics. Exaggeration sometimes helps convey the traits of a character. If your character is strong, draw him not just muscular but super buff. Think of how it looks in anime when a strong character is painted unrealistically muscular.

Convey the words or thoughts of the character. Your character might say something important or interesting if you are drawing a drawing for someone, such as mom or dad. Words can also show the traits of a character.

DO YOU WANT TO TAKE A BOOK ON A TRIP?

Bring some heavy paper with you or a piece of cardboard to bear down on for drawing when there is no table.

Store pencils and markers in a pencil case to keep them from scattering in your bag.

When you fold open the book, use a clip/clothespin to keep it from closing on its own

If you get tired of drawing, come up with stories for the characters in the book. Which of them is good or evil, who is friends with whom? Think of where they live. What is their favorite food? What do they like to do, and what don't they like. Name the characters in the book after places or cities you drive through.

If you run out of drawing paper, you can color in the characters from the book as well as add details and background to them. But be sure to put something dense between the pages if you draw with felt-tip pens. Otherwise, the felt-tip pen may bleed through to the bottom page.

HOW TO MAKE A SIMPLE POSTCARD

Do you want to make someone close to you happy? Give them a postcard, do not wait for a birthday or a holiday, but give it to them right now, and they will be very pleased.

In order to make a postcard, it is advisable to use thick paper, but if it isn't there, then you can make it out of plain paper. Take a clean sheet. Measure with a ruler 8 by 6 inches. And cut the sheet of paper.

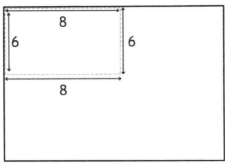

Now fold the cut sheet in half.

On the front side, draw something kind and beautiful. You can draw something from this book.

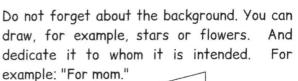

Or make a drawing on colored paper, cut out a rectangle and paste it on the front of the card.

Do not forget about the background. You can draw, for example, stars or flowers. And dedicate it to whom it is intended. For example: "For mom."

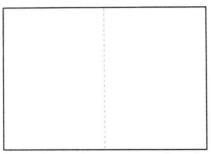

Now we need to write a wish inside our postcard, and we can draw something cute.
Write: "I love you." And draw a heart, flower, or smiley. Don't forget to color it in.
Here are some more examples of phrases you can write:
"To the best mom;"
"With love for dad;"
"Beloved grandmother;"
"To the biggest-hearted grandfather".

PAINTING ON PEBBLES

Find a smooth, flat stone. Do not take ones too large, as they can be heavy. Light-colored stones are best; you can draw a sketch on them with a pencil and then paint.

Wash the stone well with a sponge or brush from all sides. Wait for it to dry.

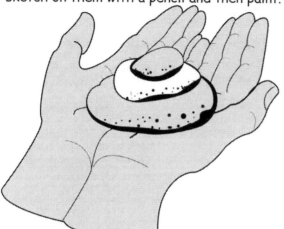

Think of what you will draw on it. The shape of the stone can give an idea for the drawing. For example, a ladybug, a bee, or a worm. It is best to color with paints, but you can use felt-tip pens or helium pens.

Pebbles like these can be given as gifts or kept as a keepsakes.

GAME: "DRAW AND PASS"

This game will help you have fun and develop your imagination. Play with your family or friends. You need at least two to play.

On a piece of paper, draw the top of your fictional character, such as the head and neck. Wrap the sheet so that you cannot see what you have drawn, but you can see where you need to start drawing. Pass the sheet to the next player. Don't say what you've drawn.

The next player draws a part of the character, wraps the sheet so that what he drew is not visible and gives it to you. He also doesn't have to tell you which character he is drawing. Now you need to guess what has already been drawn, continue drawing, and give it to the second player.

And so finish drawing, wrap and transfer the drawing until you finish the character. Then expand the drawing and see what happens. For the first time, you can agree that you are drawing a little man.

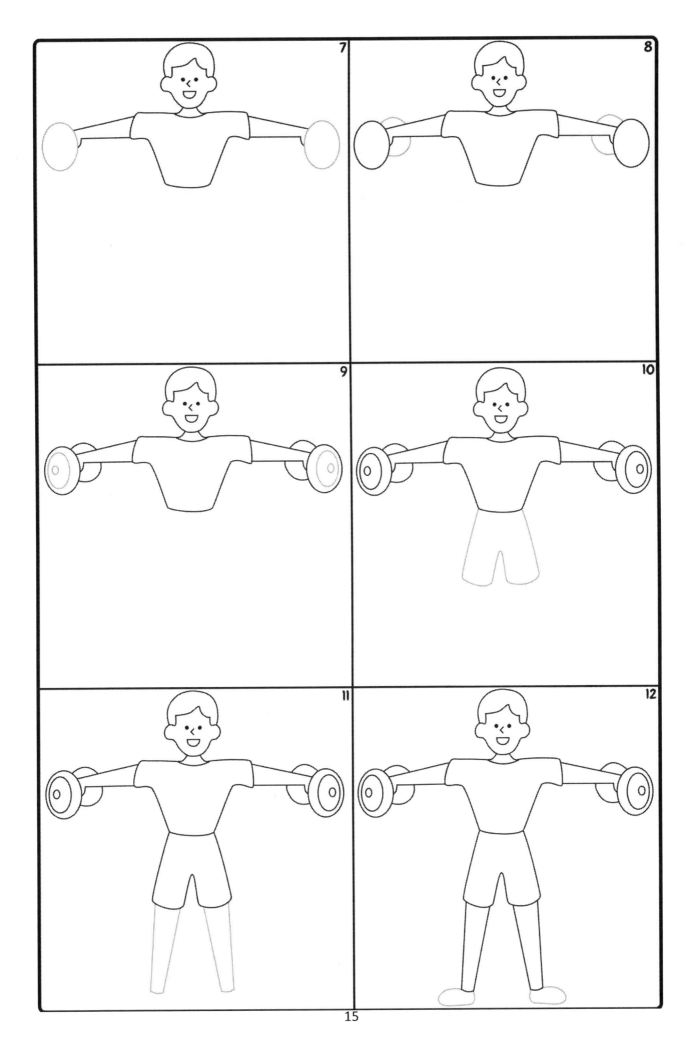

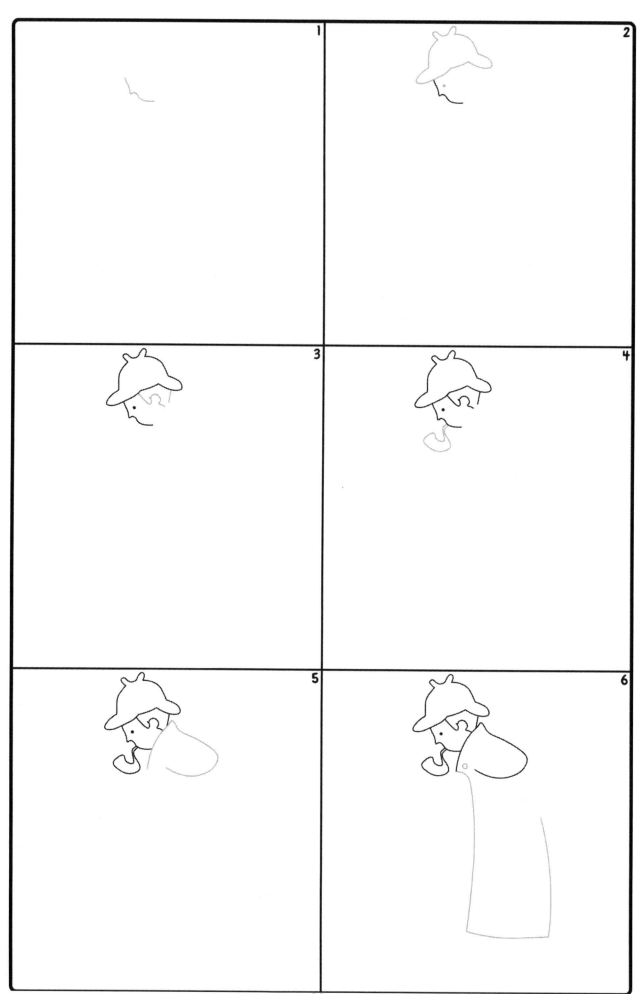

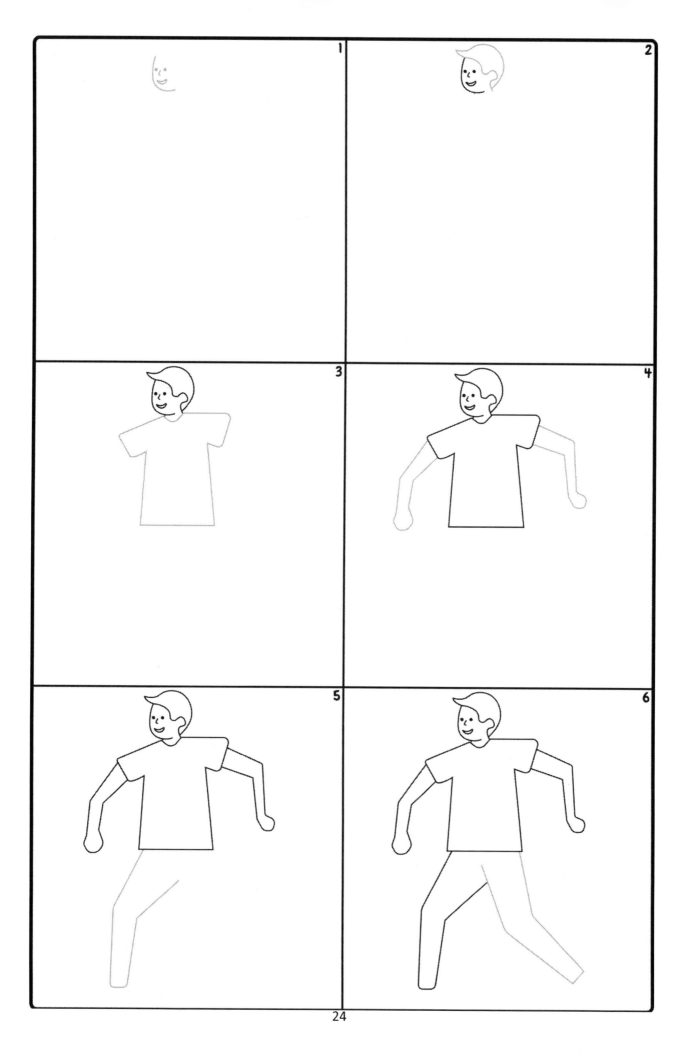

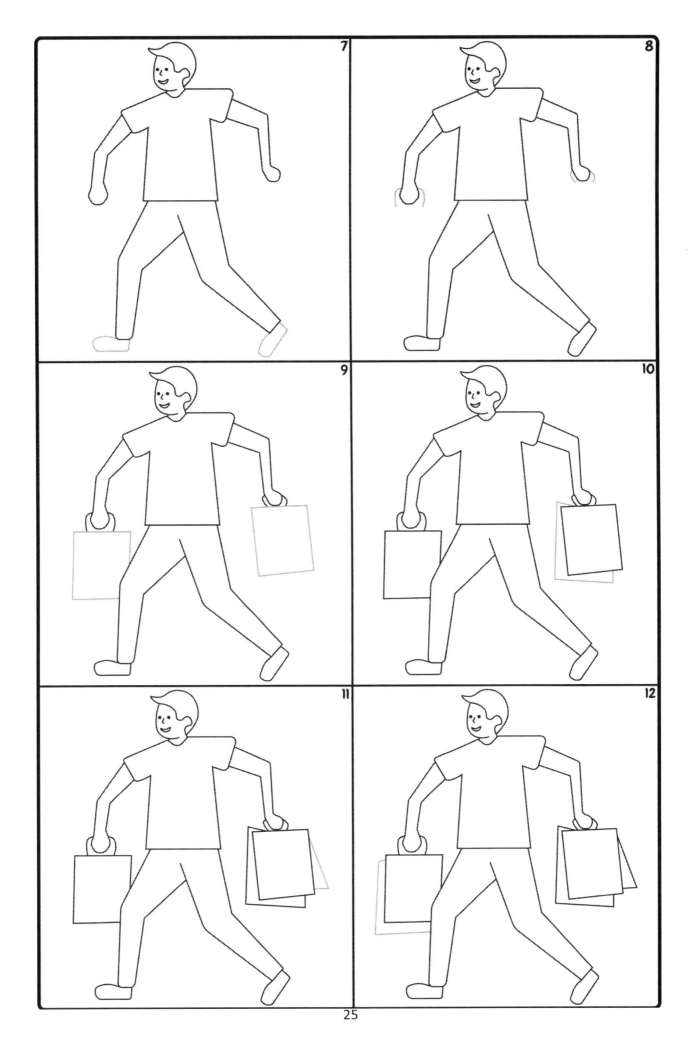

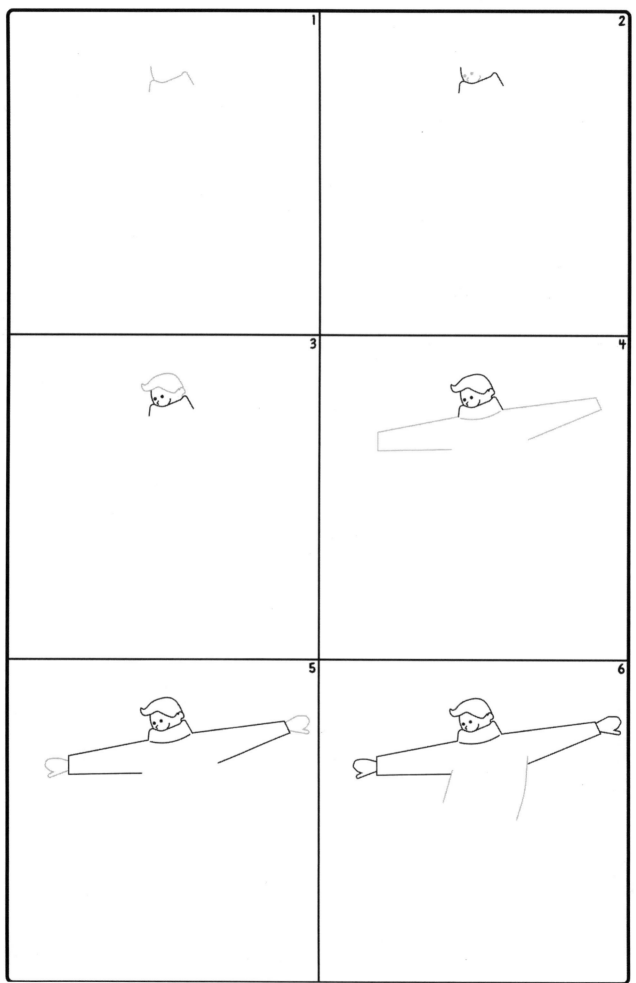

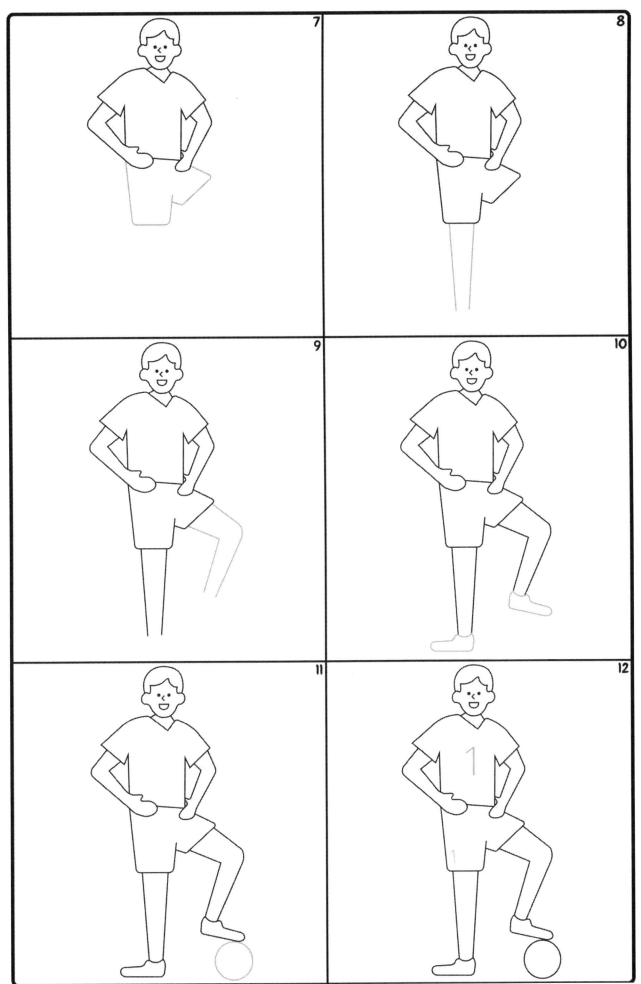

38

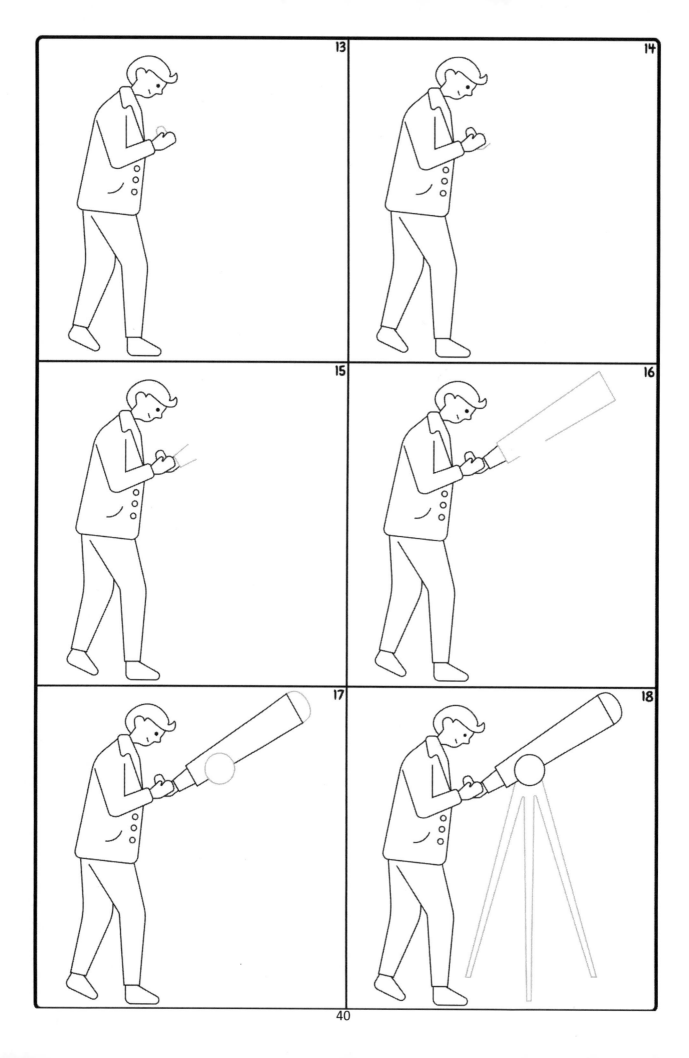

41

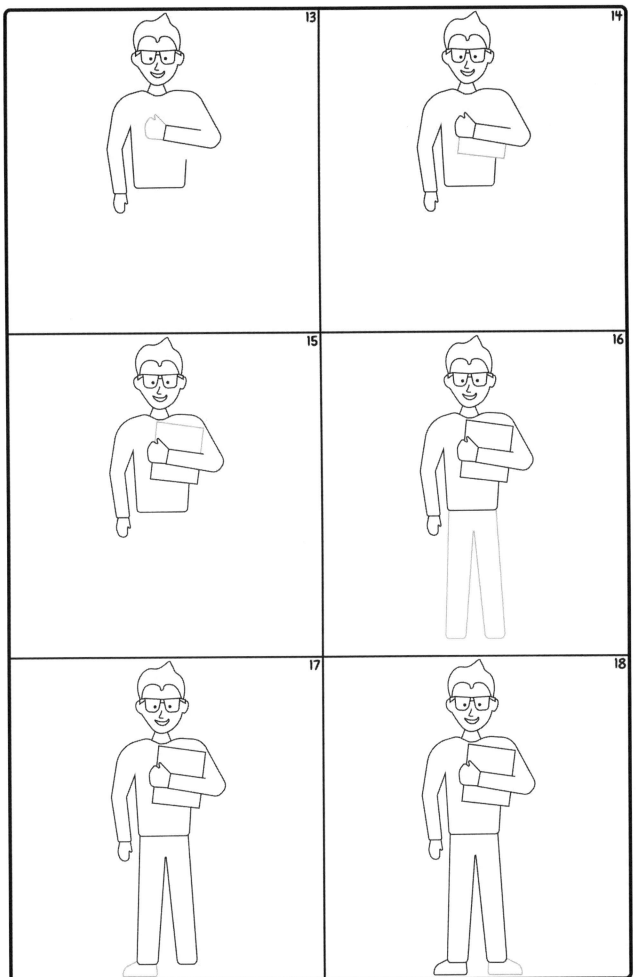

1	2
3	4
5	6

50

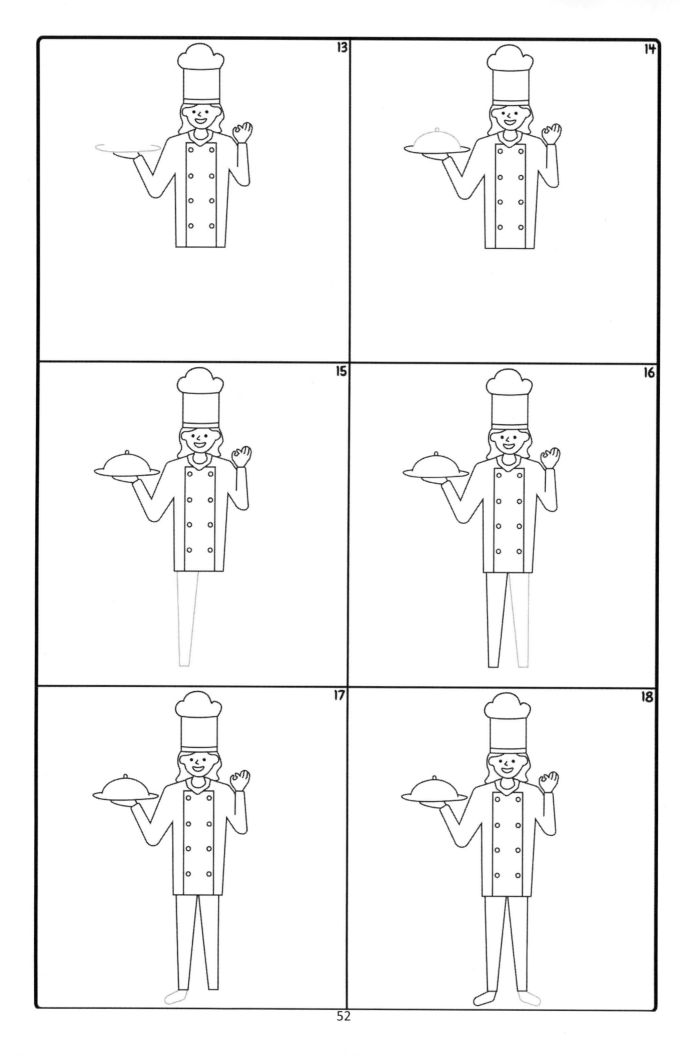

53

59

64

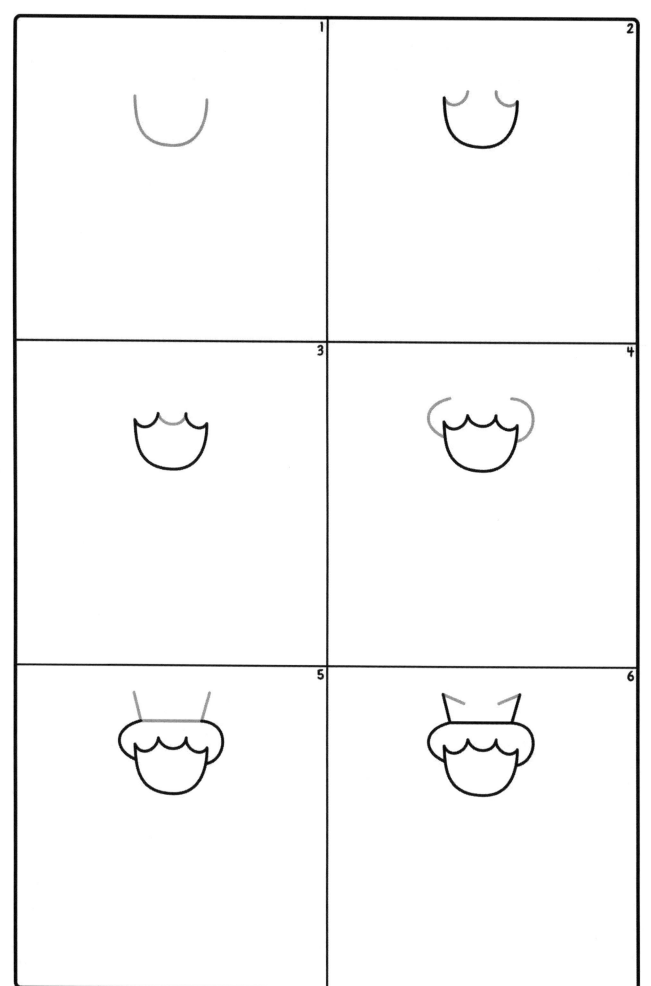

74

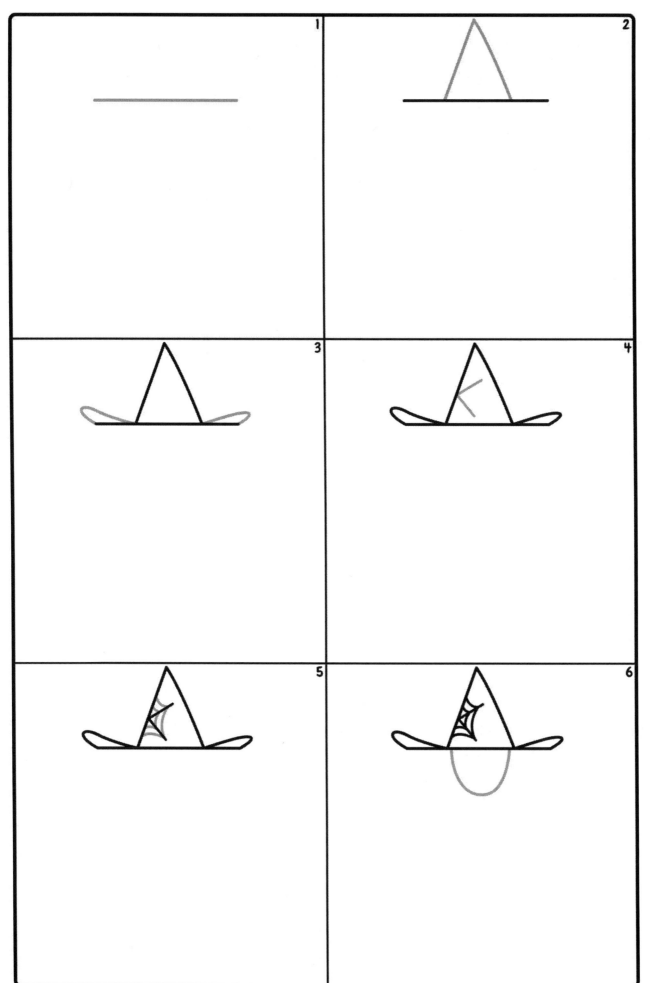

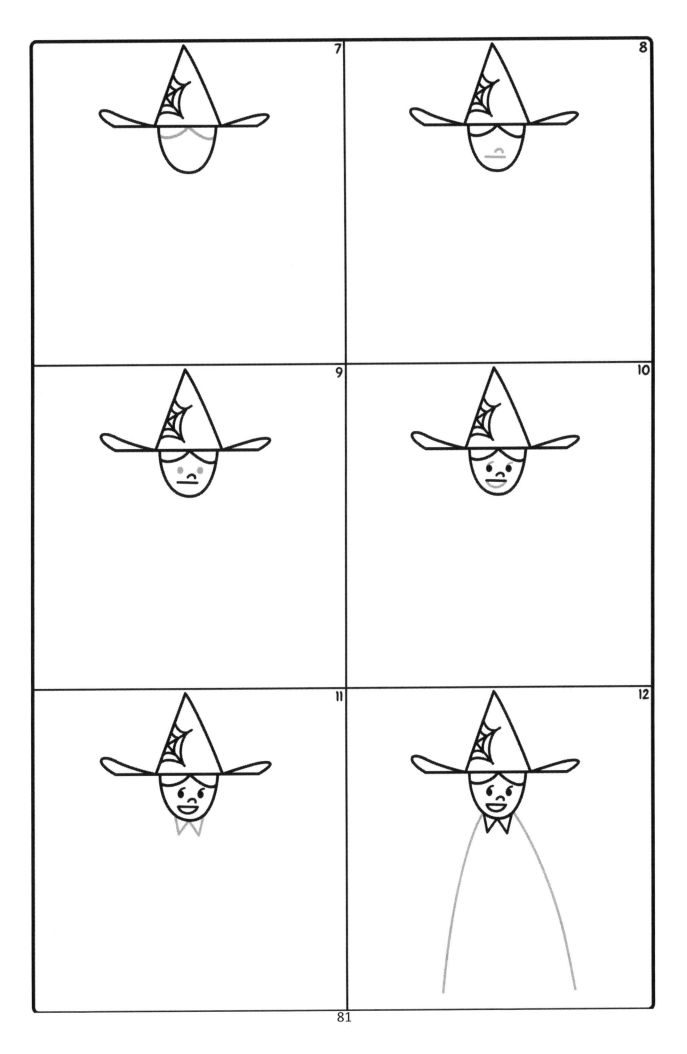

85

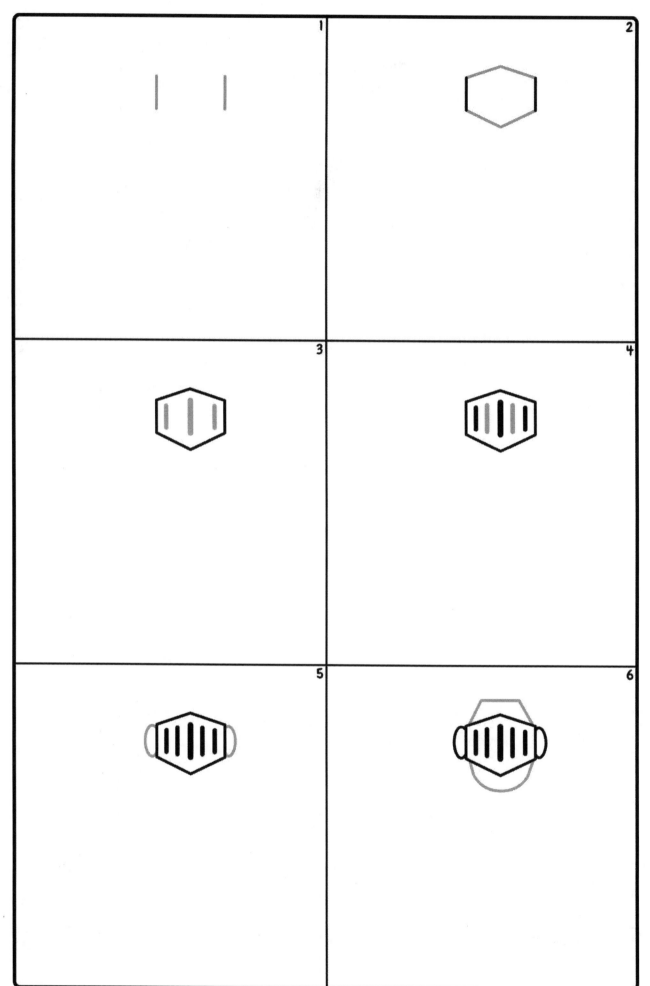

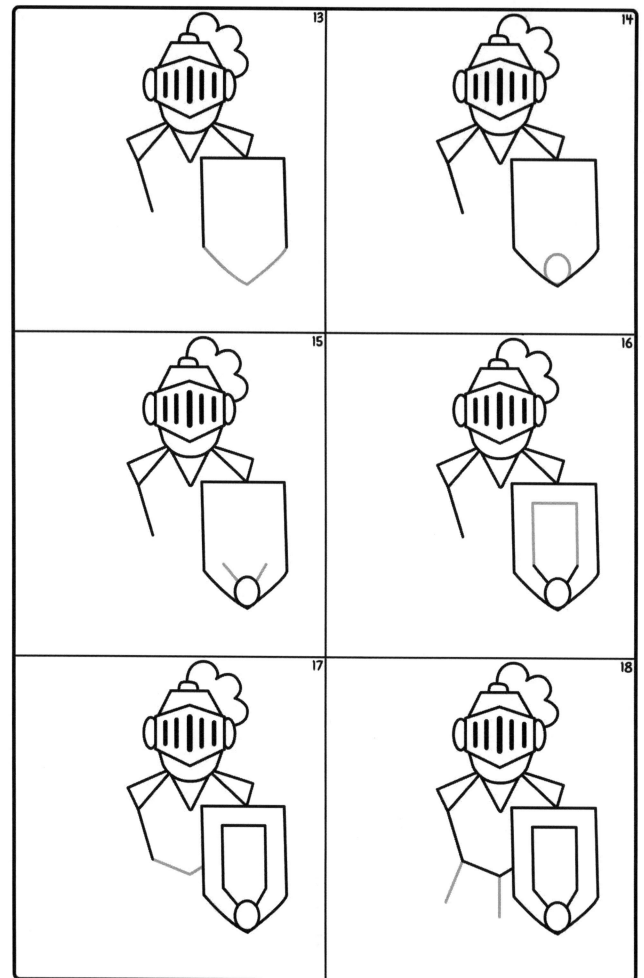

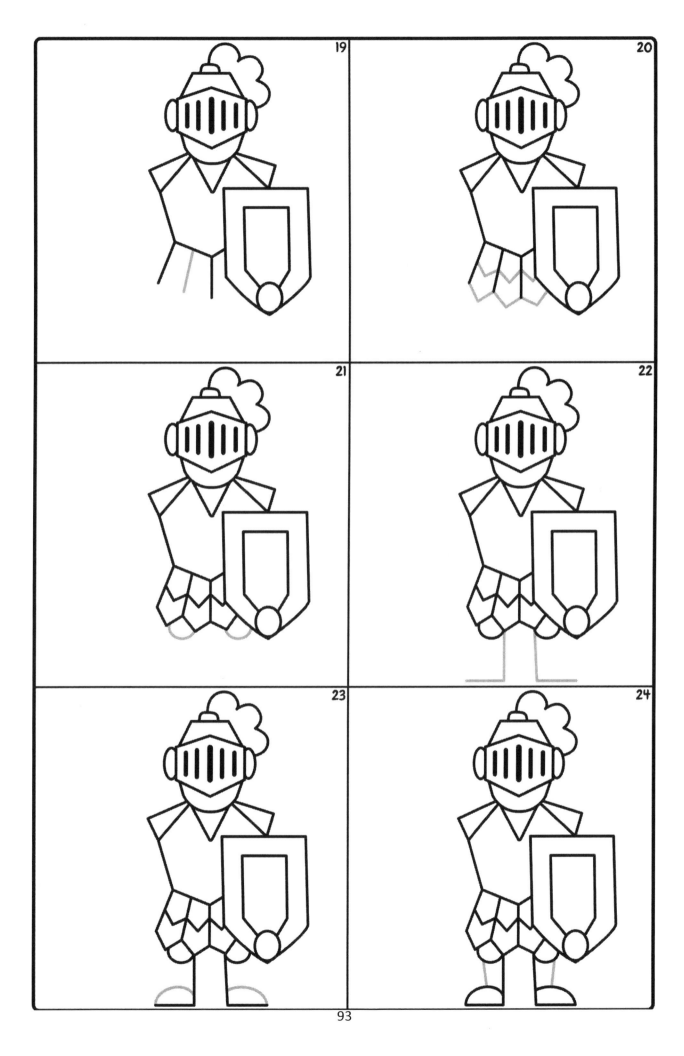

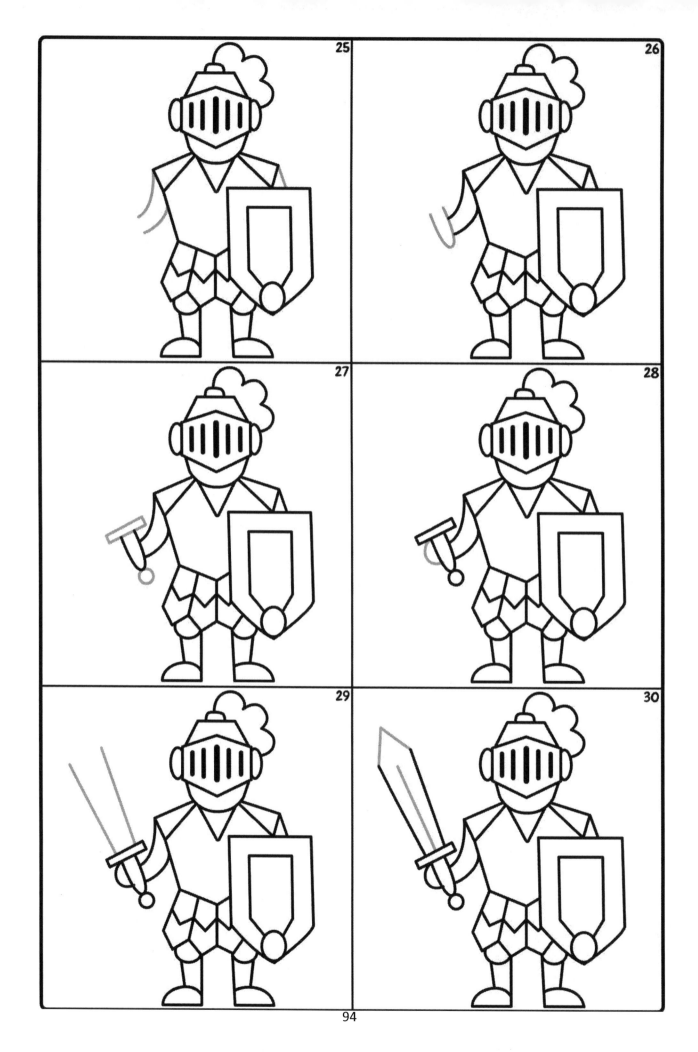

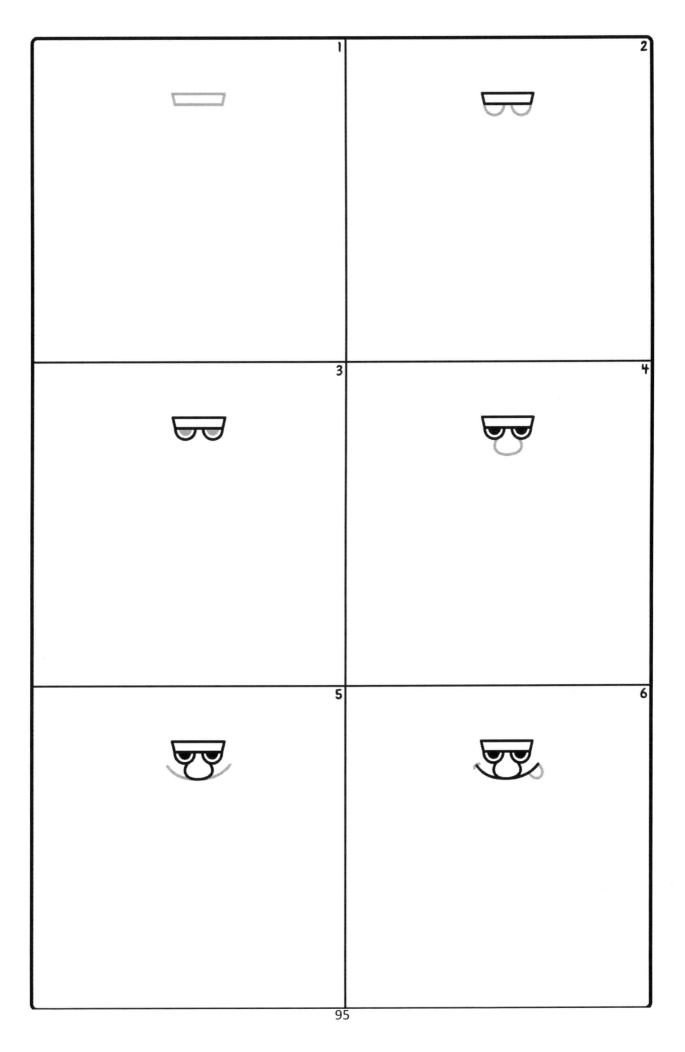

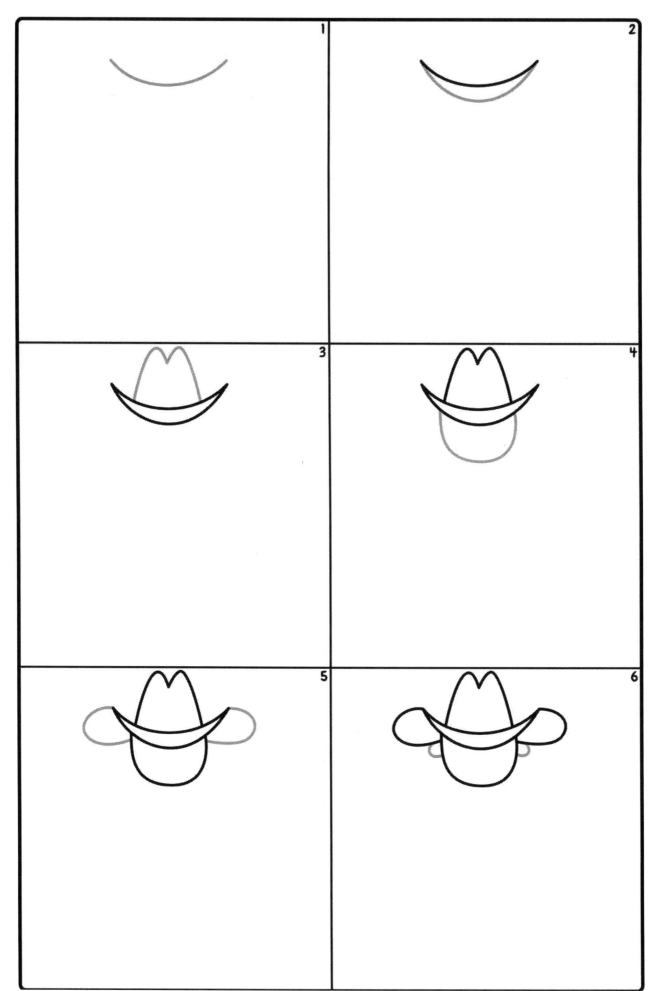

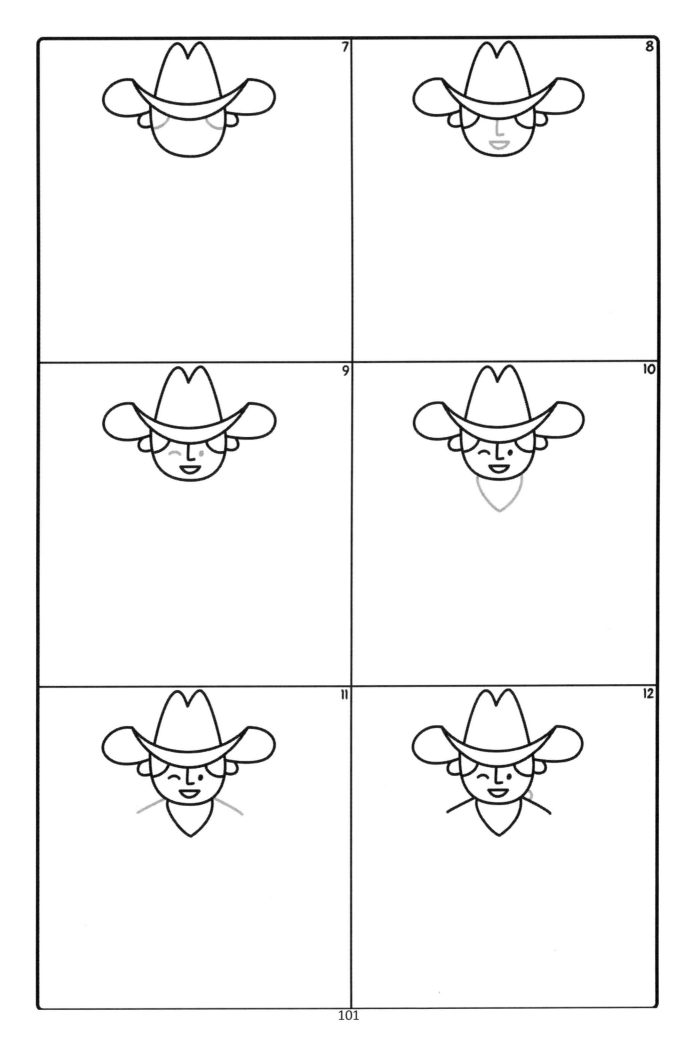